SPIDER MAN

A NATURE LOVER INTRODUCES US TO HIS SPECIAL FRIENDS

Spiders Are Special

Whenever you see a spider, remember that for many thousands of years other people have watched them, too. Like you, they have wondered about the things spiders do — things that neither you nor I could possibly manage.

In Africa, people tell a story that shows how special spiders are. In the beginning, the story goes, all the animals in the world were male. They longed to have wives, but all the female animals were goddesses, and they were up in heaven. How could the lonely male animals on earth ever get to know them?

Only the spider could help them. He made a great ladder of silk, stretching high into the clouds, and led the other animals into heaven. The animals found their wives among the goddesses. But

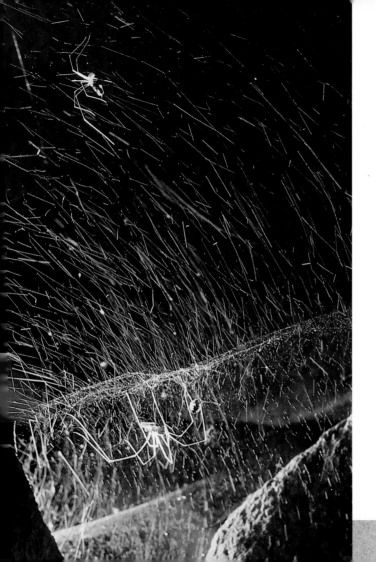

before they returned to earth, one animal, the hare, stole some food. The theft was soon discovered, and all the animals blamed the spider.

The spider said nothing to defend himself, for he was too hurt to speak. But when the animals were back on earth, the spider took away his silk ladder so no one could find the way to heaven again.

Many other stories tell how unfairly spiders have been treated. Make sure you don't do the same.

Meet My Friends

Now I'm going to introduce you to my friends the spiders. First, though, you need to realize that spiders' faces differ considerably.

Nearly all spiders have eight eyes, which can be arranged in a variety of ways. Spiders which build webs have small eyes and often cannot see very well.

Many web-building spiders have four eyes in the middle of their faces and two on either side, like this brown garden spider.

Some spiders have all their eyes in one cluster on top of their heads, like this tarantula, a funnel-web spider.

Hunting spiders don't make webs for catching their food. Instead, they run after insects, or stalk them. They need at least two really big eyes to help them see clearly.

Other hunting spiders, like this long-haired forest spider, have four large eyes and two smaller ones.

Many hunting spiders have two big eyes in front and six smaller ones in different positions, like this jumping spider.

Try bending over a jumping spider and blinking slowly. Spiders can't blink, and jumping spiders find eyes fascinating. They will often look up and wonder who you are.

Spinning Silk

When I was a boy, I used to sit for hours watching my favorite garden spider go around and around, spinning her spiral. We call this kind of web an orb-web. Some spiders spin simple sheets of silk. Others spin intricate towers.

This male cave spider uses his spinnerets, on the left of the photograph, to weave a tunnel around himself.

Most spiders use their spinnerets, at the rear of their bodies, to spin their webs.

When they want to spin themselves a safe hideaway to sleep in, spiders spin a much softer sort of silk. Most mother spiders also spin bags for their eggs. We call these egg sacs.

I often find spiders' egg sacs, some of them covered with brightly colored silk. Here is one I found recently. At first I thought the threads were pure gold.

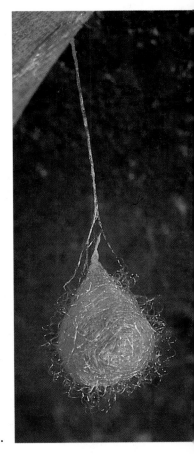

Good Vibrations

Try to imagine what it must be like to hear through your fingers and toes! Spiders don't have ears to hear with. Instead, they feel vibrations through their eight legs.

Do you know what a tuning fork is? I always carry one in my pocket when I go looking for spiders. I use it as a front doorbell on their webs. Once, when I was walking along some cliffs, I saw an enormous web. I struck the tuning fork on my knee to make it ring, and then touched it on the web. At once, a large black spider came hurtling down and began biting the tuning fork angrily.

Many male spiders of the black widow family know about front doorbells, too. When one wants a female to become his mate, he starts plucking at her web, as if he were playing a harp. If the female does not want the male's company, she will rush down and chase him away. But if she is feeling friendly, she will walk slowly down into the middle of her web, spinning a path of special silk behind her. If she waits until the male's serenade has finished, he knows that it is safe to enter the web.

Other Ways of Hunting

I once watched a big jumping spider hunting his prey. When he saw a fly on the wall above him, he approached it and began waving his feelers up and down. Suddenly the fly had had enough. It flew off — straight into the spider's jaws! Usually, jumping spiders stalk their prey then leap on it. But this one seemed to have worked out a smarter system!

Some of the most colorful spiders are the crab spiders. They are brightly colored because they usually hunt by imitating parts of flowers. They just stand still and wait for their prey to come to them.

Look at this crab spider, which I found on a hawksbeard flower. See how her yellow face and green legs match the colors of the plant?

Close relatives of the little crab spiders are the large huntsman spiders, which are actually among the most friendly and harmless of all. This huge white huntsman spider, with brilliant red jaws, is one of the most magnificent I have seen.

Spiders from Long Ago

The spiders I find most fascinating are two kinds of tarantulas — the funnel-web spiders and the trapdoor spiders. There were very similar spiders in the earliest forests of the world, even before the dinosaurs. Tarantulas look very different from other spiders. Their jaws stand straight out in front of their faces, while the jaws of ordinary spiders are usually below their heads.

Tarantulas have huge fangs which face backwards under the jaws, but are brought forward when the spider is preparing to strike. Most other spiders have tiny fangs which face into each other.

Another difference
is that tarantulas live
much longer than
ordinary spiders.

I encouraged this purse-web tarantula to show her fangs to the camera by gently blowing into her face through a straw. (I don't recommend that you try this.)

Most spiders live for between one and two years. But this funnel-web spider can live for twenty years or more.

Mothers and Babies

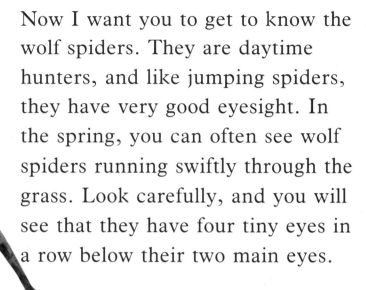

Now I want you to get to know the wolf spiders. They are daytime hunters, and like jumping spiders, they have very good eyesight. In the spring, you can often see wolf spiders running swiftly through the grass. Look carefully, and you will see that they have four tiny eyes in a row below their two main eyes.

Female wolf spiders are very good mothers. Like other spiders, they spin a round egg sac. Once it is finished, they attach it to their spinnerets.

When the eggs hatch, the wolf spider's babies climb on her back. She carries them around for several weeks, until they are old enough to look after themselves.

A wolf spider mother will never leave her egg sac unguarded for a single moment.

Mothers and Babies

I never get tired of watching female spiders spin their delicate egg sacs. Sometimes the eggs themselves are brightly colored. I have seen egg sacs which are rust-brown, blue, and green.

Spiders of the black widow family are excellent mothers. They keep their babies in the web — often a

A shiny black spider, a harmless relative of the black widow, laid these soft pink eggs in my garden last year.

hundred or more at one time. The mother feeds each one separately, by chewing up food and putting it in the baby's mouth. This is why many people call black widows "mothering" spiders.

But not all spiders get the chance to be good mothers. Many of the spiders which spin orb-webs don't live for more than a few hours after their eggs are laid. They use all their energy laying the eggs and spinning the sac, and then die while guarding their eggs.

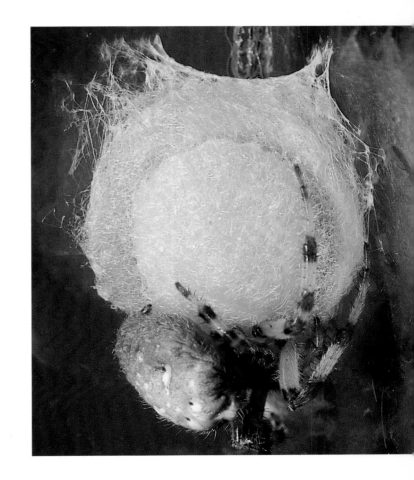

Growing Up

Most of us do not think about growing — it just happens. But for spiders, growing presents quite a problem. A spider's skin cannot grow, so how can it get bigger? The spider has to take its skin right off, and with eight long legs that is a difficult task! The colors of the new skin underneath are often brighter for a few hours.

Here is a tiny baby of the mothering spider family. She is only 1.5 mm (0.06 in) long. Every time she shed her skin, she lost more and more of her white coloration, as the black dots began to link up.

By the time she was 5 mm (0.2 in) long, there were only a few white stripes left, and a blotchy brown stripe had appeared down her back. I thought she had reached her adult coloring, but I was wrong.

About three weeks later, she shed her skin again. The brown blotches had grown into a smooth, orange pattern framed by white. Apart from that, she was a glistening jet black.

Spiders in the Air

I have seen some very strange things in the world of spiders. Once I watched a jumping spider that danced in time to music! But the most astonishing thing of all was the spider that walked through the air.

I was exploring some woodland when I noticed a spider walking

On sunny days, baby spiders can sometimes be seen doing handstands on their front legs. Look closely and you will see them release a delicate thread. When a warm air current tugs at the thread, the spider will float up and away.

across the path — about 1 m (3 ft) above the ground. I moved my hand cautiously around in front of it, to see if it was following a thread too thin for me to see. But it made no difference.

Probably the spider was using a warm air current to stay off the ground. Spiders can travel long distances on air currents, especially crab spiders, which are clumsy walkers.

I put this crab spider on a red blossom so that you can see its face clearly.

How Safe Are Spiders?

Like most animals, spiders are not likely to bite you unless you frighten them. But if you do get bitten, there are several important things to do. First, capture the spider so you can show it to the doctor, who will need to know what sort of spider it is. Next, put an ice pack on the bite. And above all, keep calm. The bite will almost certainly not do you any serious harm, but it is worth a visit to the doctor to make sure.

A big jar can make a home for small spiders, but large ones need an old aquarium, perhaps with some earth or sand, a few plants, and a piece of wood or cork.

Spiders can make interesting pets. They do not need feeding every day, but you should feed most spiders at least once a week, always with live insects. Spiders will not eat pieces of meat or pet food. You should also soak some cotton in water and leave it in the spider's home. It will prefer to suck the water out rather than drink from a bowl.

And remember, if you begin neglecting your spiders, it's time to let them go.

Some spiders, like this one my wife Jane is holding, love to have their hairy bodies stroked. Take care not to get any hair in your eyes as it is irritating.

Photo Index

You may like to know where the spiders shown in this book live. This index will also tell you the scientific name for each spider's family.